SHIP TO SHORE:

LEARN TO HAVE FUN USING MORSE CODE!

A Guide to Learning Morse Code Using Visual Clues

BY SUSAN FERRIS RIGHTS

Copyright © 2012 Susan Ferris Rights
All rights reserved
ISBN 978-0-9858005-0-5

The Morse Code

Invented in 1844 by an American named Samuel F. B. Morse (April 27, 1791 – April 2, 1872), Morse Code is an internationally used code made of dots and dashes in various combinations that stand for individual letters and numbers.

Morse Code Sounder

It is widely used, and can be sent in many ways, making it very useful. It can be sent by a whistle, buzzer, tapping, flags, lights, and by clenching and opening a hand.

Traditionally, it was used in radio telegraphy, but is now used mostly by amateur (ham) radio operators. Today most ship-to-shore communications use satellite transmissions.

A Brief History of the Development of Wireless Communication

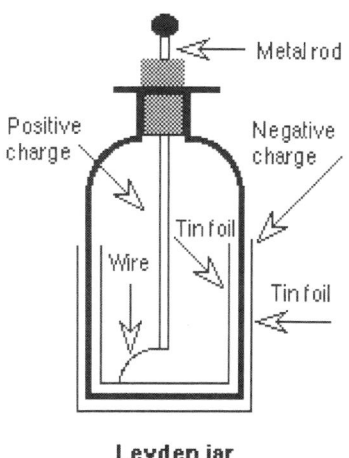

Leyden jar

Before there was wireless communication a other means of communication had already been developed. One of the first was developed by Charles Morrison, in 1753. This involved sending messages through 26 insulated electrical wires.

These conducting charges caused movements in small pieces of paper on which each letter of the alphabet was written. The attracted paper determined the letter being transmitted.

His system of using these 26 wires, one for each letter of the alphabet, and many Leyden jars (see Figure 1) was complex and prone to many errors. In addition, this method of communication could only be used over very short distances.

Ten years later, Bosolus reduced the wires needed down to only two by using a letter code.

Meanwhile after studying and painting in France and Italy, Samuel F. B. Morse traveled from Europe to America. Part of Morse's interest in improved communications was quite personal in nature. At the time of the death of his first wife. Morse, at the age of 25, was away from home. The news of her death took 2 weeks to reach him!

Morse soon learned about European discoveries regarding electromagnetic properties and made his first notes regarding his "Recording Electric Magnetic Telegraph" and a dot - dash alphabet code.

Morse's apparatus, that used a printer's "port rule" with cast type, was publicly demonstrated in January of 1838. Each letter of type had saw teeth filed in the edge to activate the sending machine. A letter's code symbol length was based upon the various quantities of type found in the printer's office. The register (receiver) was an electromagnet-activated pen, drawing the saw tooth symbols on a thin strip of moving paper.

Then, Samuel F. B. Morse invented the telegraph, which uses an electromagnet. Together with his partner Alfred Vail, Morse developed in 1838 the simple operator key. When this key was depressed it completed an electrical circuit and sent a signal to a distant receiver. An electromagnet moved a marker that embossed a series of dots and dashes (the Morse Code) on a paper roll (patent No.1647).

On January 24, 1838 Morse demonstrated his telegraph over a ten-mile circuit at New York University. Transmission speed was recorded at 10 words-per-minute.

One month later he demonstrated the telegraph to President Martin Van Buren and his cabinet. Congressman Francis O.J. Smith recognized the possibilities and becomes interested. On April 6 Smith delivered a Congressional report on Morse's Telegraph Bill.

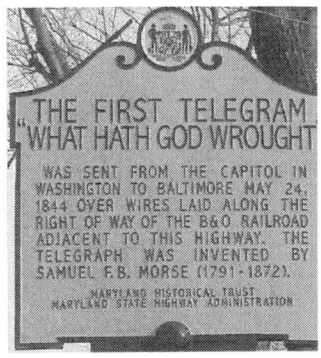

Once Morse convinced Congress to sanction the first long-distance telegraph line, an iron wire was strung between posts from Baltimore, Maryland to Washington, D.C. -- a distance of 37 miles. On May 24, 1844, the first telegraph message, "What hath God wrought," was successfully sent and received along the first telegraph wire system.

About 1856 a sounding key was developed that enabled operators to hear the message clicks and write or type it directly down in plain language.

Telegraph systems quickly spread across Europe and the United States. With the growing telegraph traffic many improvements followed.

How the Telegraph Works.

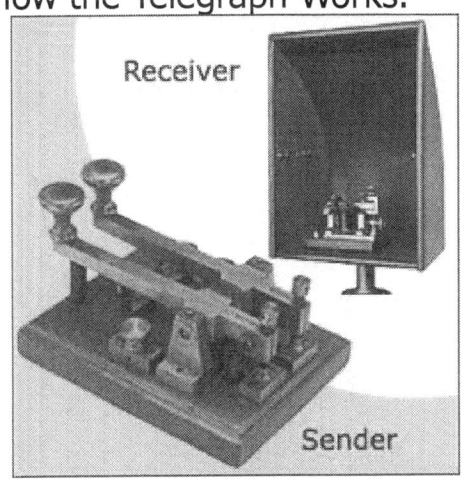

When the sender taps the key, a circuit is closed and an electric current is delivered to the sounder.

The sounder operates by giving distinct sounds (like clicks) or a paper is tapped and the message is received. The message has to be decoded for it to be understood.

In 1876, Alexander Graham Bell experimented with the telegraph and found a means to eliminate the coding and decoding of messages. He developed the telephone that allowed sounds to be transmitted over the wires. Figure 3 shows how this is done.

How the Early Telephone Worked

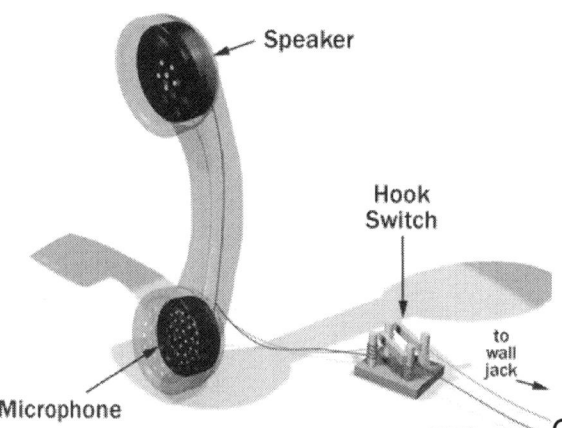

Carbon granules are contained in the microphone and are connected to the telephone circuit. When one speaks on the microphone, the sound waves of the voice compress and decompress the granules resulting to changing of the resistance in the wire which is a pattern of variation. When the current reaches the receiving station, the speaker, on the other hand, converts this electrical energy back to sound energy with the corresponding sound pattern.

Wires are no longer used in most of today's communication. Remember cell phones? Communication now is "wireless". There is no need to connect the transmitting and receiving stations. Energy is transmitted through space!

The Transatlantic Cable

By 1858, transatlantic cables between Europe and America had been laid, although these suffered many breakages. In some ways, this was the first Internet. Interestingly, in 1867, along with Alexander Bell's famous invention of the telephone, the U.S. bought Russian America (now Alaska) from Russia partly in order to lay a telegraph line through the Bering Strait to Europe, although the eventual success of the trans-Atlantic cable in 1868 meant this never went ahead.

Thomas Edison developed the first successful electric lamp a few years later, and in 1883 demonstrated his "Edison effect" and patented the first diode. Five years later, German Heinrich Hertz discovered radio waves, and by 1894 Italian physicist, Guglielmo Marconi was sending radio transmissions ¾ of a mile, and within three years, the Marconi Company demonstrated long-range ship to shore radio communications. The radio revolution had begun!

http://www.netvalley.com/internet_history-right1.htm
http://nedmartin.org/uni/COMP1800/history-telecoms.html
http://www.privateline.com/mt_telephonehistory/ii_early_telephone_development/
http://www.sparkmuseum.com/TELEGRAPH.HTM

Morse Code Letters

A ● —		N — ●	
B — ● ● ●		O — — —	
C — ● — ●		P ● — — ●	
D — ● ●		Q — — ● —	
E ●		R ● — ●	
F ● ● — ●		S ● ● ●	
G — — ●		T —	
H ● ● ● ●		U ● ● —	
I ● ●		V ● ● ● —	
J ● — — —		W ● — —	
K — ● —		X — ● ● —	
L ● — ● ●		Y — ● — —	
M — —		Z — — ● ●	

Morse Code Numbers

0 — — — — —	5 ● ● ● ● ●
1 ● — — — —	6 — ● ● ● ●
2 ● ● — — —	7 — — ● ● ●
3 ● ● ● — —	8 — — — ● ●
4 ● ● ● ● —	9 — — — — ●

A ● —

Alligator

B — ● ● ●

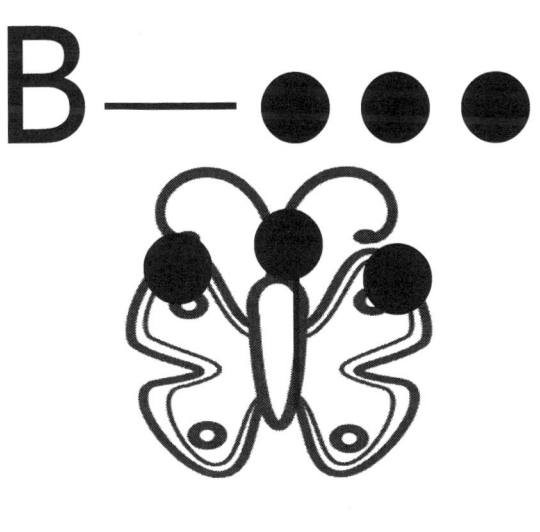

Butterfly

C

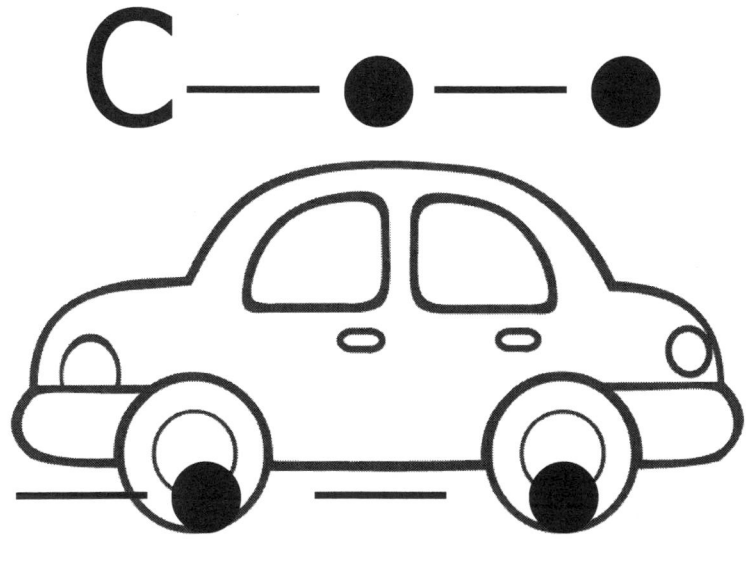

Car

D

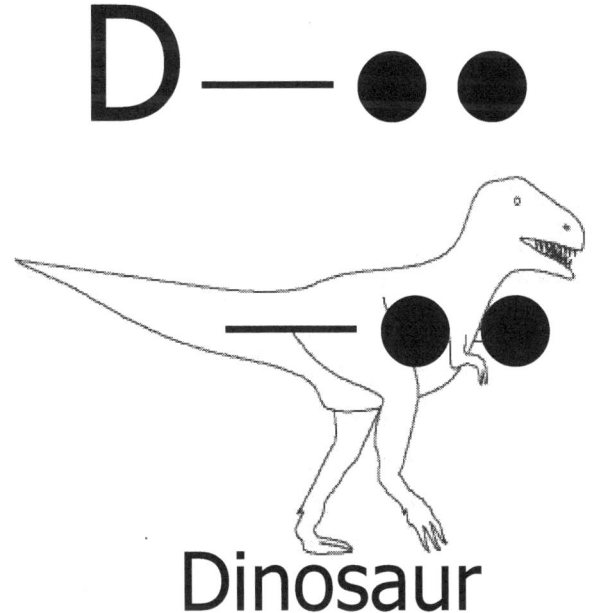

Dinosaur

E ●

Egg

F ● ● — ●

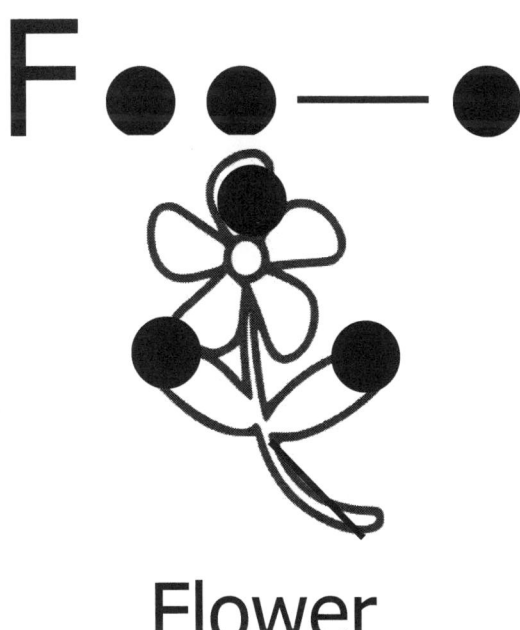

Flower

G

Gecko

H ● ● ● ●

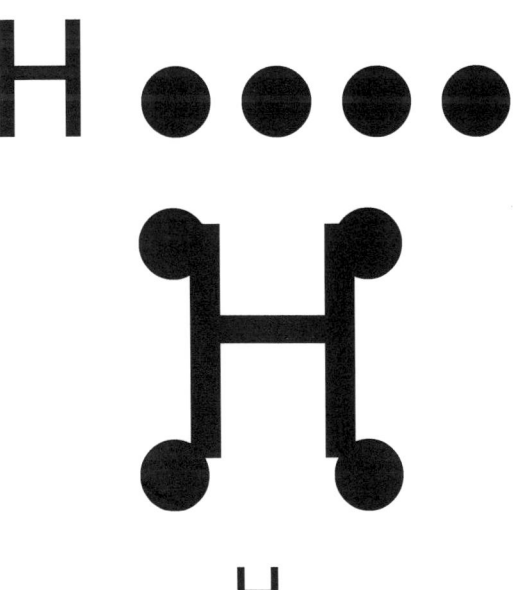

H

I ● ●

I love ice cream

J● ─ ─ ─ ─

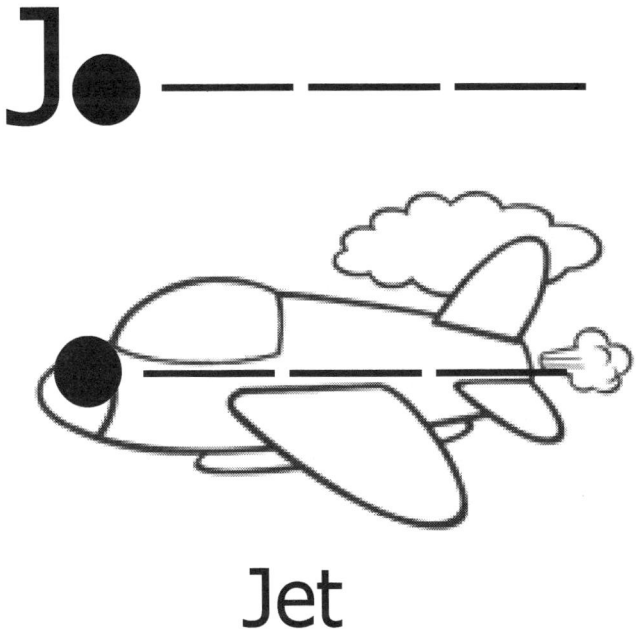

Jet

K —●—

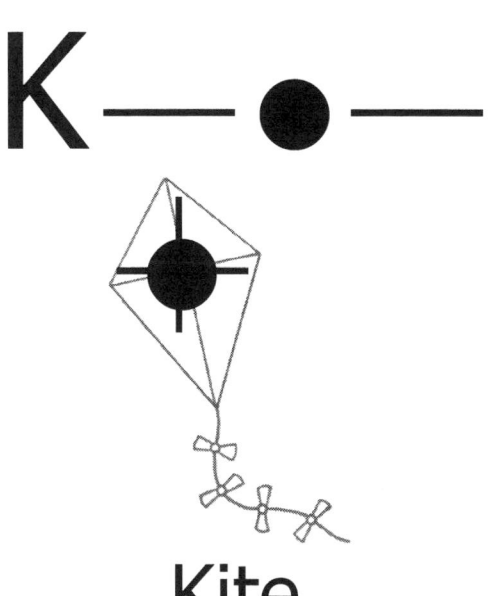

Kite

L●—●●

Lion

M — —

Money

N — •

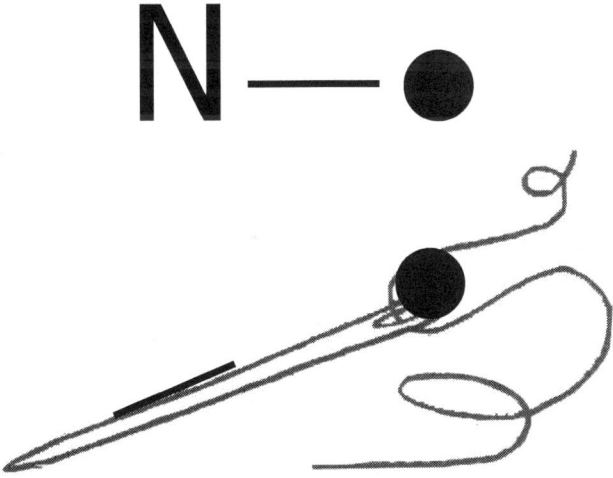

Needle

O _ _ _ _

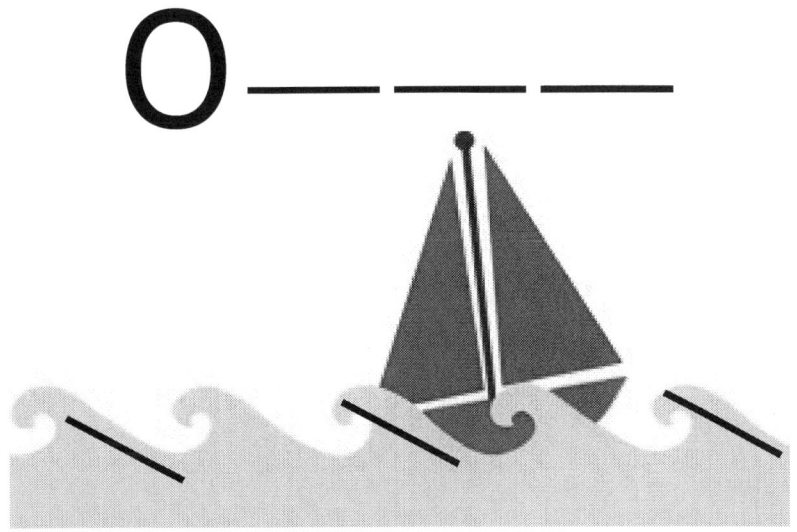

Ocean

P _ _ _ _

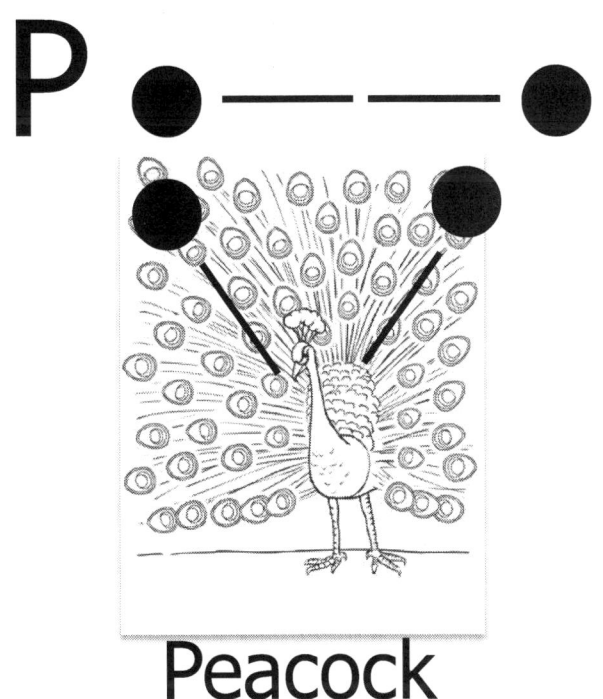

Peacock

Q — — • —

Quack! Quack!

R • — •

Rabbit

S ●●●

Snowflakes

T—

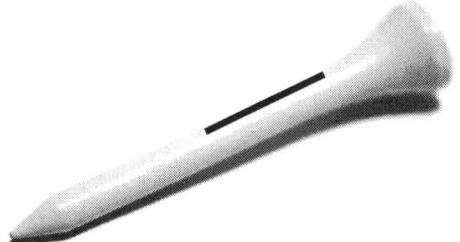

Tee

U ●● —

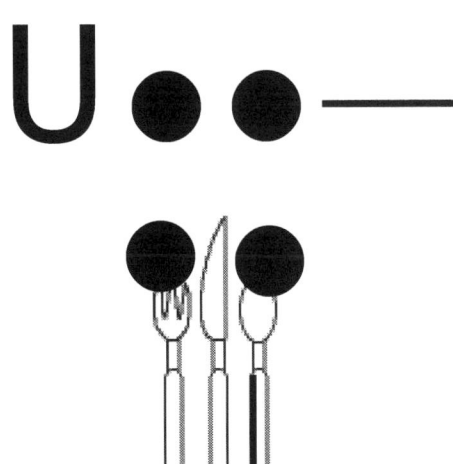

Utensils

V ●●● —

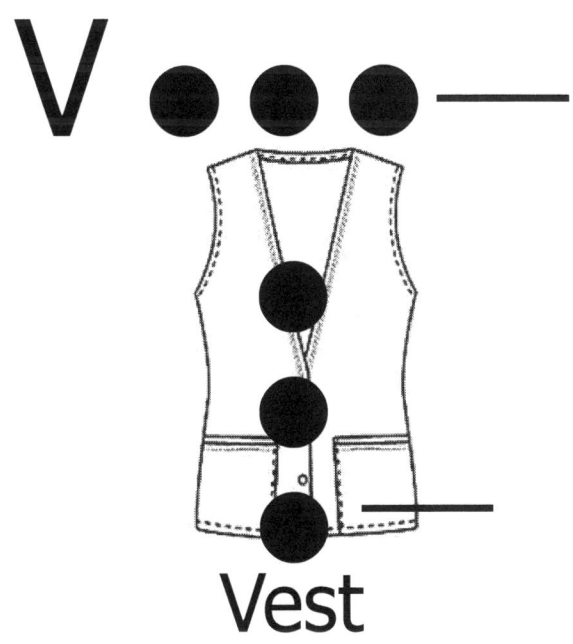

Vest

W •———

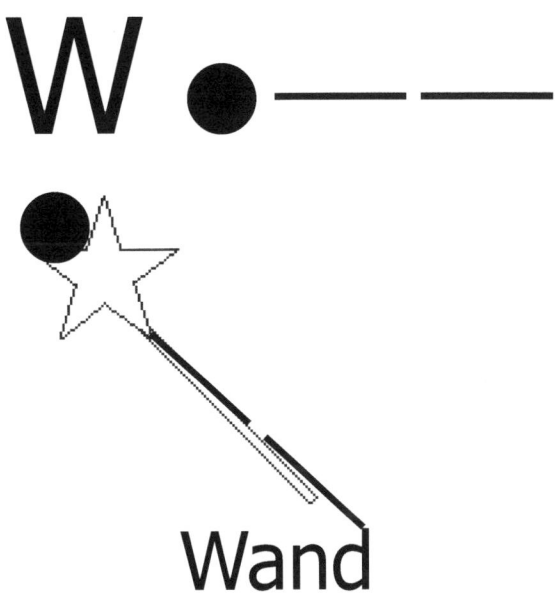

Wand

X—•• —

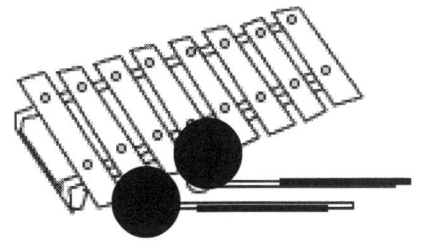

Xylophone

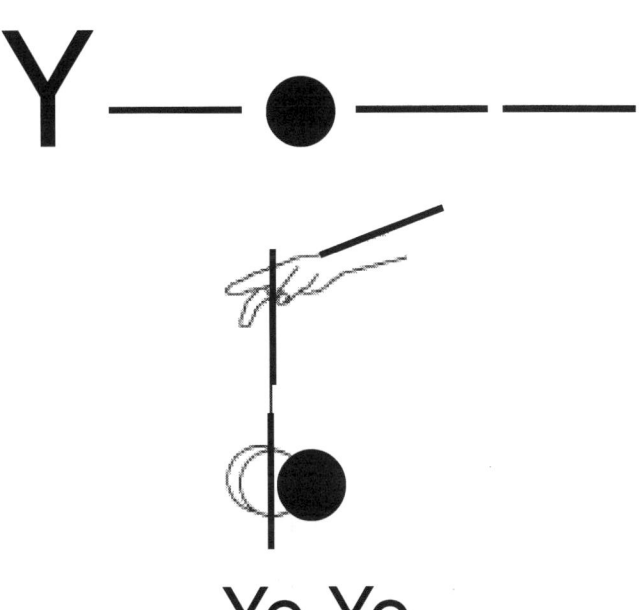

Yo-Yo

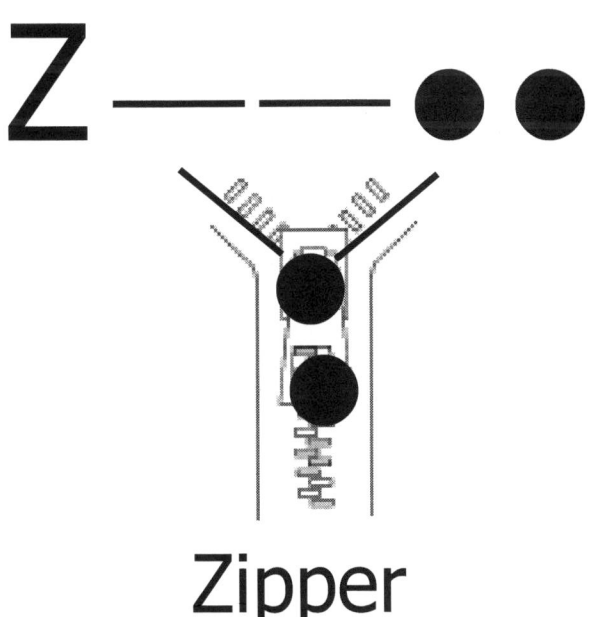

Zipper

Now see if you can de-code this message:

-.-- --- ..- / .... .- ...- . / -..
--- -. . / .- / --. .-. . .- - / .---
--- -... / .-.. . .- .-. -. .. -. --. /
-- --- .-. ... . / -.-. --- -.. . .-.-.-

Write your answer here:

YOU / HAVE / DONE / A / GREAT / JOB / LEARNING / MORSE / CODE.

You have done a great job learning Morse Code!

Using Morse Code, write your name here:

___ ___ ___ ___ ___ ___ ___ ___ ___

Using Morse Code, write your birthday here:

___ ___ ___ ___ ___ ___ ___ ___ ___ ___

___ ___ ___ ___ ___ ___ ___ ___ ___ ___

___ ___

Using Morse Code, write your address:

___ ___ ___ ___ ___ ___ ___ ___ ___ ___

___ ___ ___ ___ ___ ___ ___ ___ ___ ___

___ ___

How would you write the name of your school?

___ ___ ___ ___ ___ ___ ___ ___ ___ ___

___ ___ ___ ___ ___ ___ ___ ___ ___ ___

Can you answer these questions?
Write your answers above the code.

.-- .... .- - / .. ... / -.-- --- ..- .-. / ..-. .- ...-
--- .-. .. - . / -.-. .- -. -.. / --- ..-. / -.-. .- -.
-.. .-.- ..--..

ANSWER_____

.-- .... --- / .. ... / -.-- --- ..- .-. / -... . ... -
/ ..-. .-. .. . -. -.. ..--..

ANSWER_____

.-- .... .- - / .. ... / -.-- --- ..- .-. / ..-. .- ...-
--- .-. .. - . / .... --- .-.. .. -.. .- -.-- ..--..

ANSWER_____

HAVE FUN!

Here are some great websites for learning to work with Morse Code:

1-Morse Code Translator
http://morsecode.scphillips.com/jtranslator.html
On this site you can do the following activities:

Text to Morse
Just type letters, numbers and punctuation into the top box and press the "Translate" button. The program will place the Morse code in the bottom box, inserting a "?" if the character cannot be translated. If you are learning Morse code it is recommended that you use the "toggle" button to turn of the dots and dashes output as reading this can slow your learning down.

Morse to Text
You can type Morse code into the top box using "." for a dot and "-" or "_" for a dash. Letters are separated by spaces and words by "/" or "|". When you hit the "Translate" button the program will translate it into plain text. If it cannot translate a letter it will place a "?" in the output.

Sound
If you want to turn the sound on then use the radio buttons at the bottom. There are options to control the volume, pitch and speed. The "Farnsworth speed" is useful when learning Morse code as it can be set lower than the other speed in order to stretch out the spaces between characters and words whilst keeping the Morse characters fast.

2-Morse Code Machine
http://boyslife.org/games/online-games/575/morse-code-machine/
This is a game that both teaches and quizzes you about Morse Code

3-CSS Sam's Operation: Dit Dah
http://www.classbraingames.com/2009/12/learn-morse-code/
Learn Morse code and become a pro at deciphering messages. You never know when it might come in handy!

Use these pages to try out some of your ideas!

Use these pages to try out some of your ideas!

Use these pages to try out some of your ideas!